DON'T SPIT IN THE SOUP.
WE'VE ALL GOT TO EAT.
CHAIRMAN JOHNSON

QUOTATIONS FROM CHAIRMAN LBJ

SIMON AND SCHUSTER
NEW YORK

Published by Simon and Schuster
Rockefeller Center, 630 Fifth Avenue
New York, New York 10020

THIRD PRINTING

Library of Congress Catalog Card Number:
68-14846
Designed by Eve Metz
Manufactured in the United States of America
Printed by Mahony & Roese, Inc., New York, N.Y.
Bound by Electronic Perfect Binders, Inc.,
Brooklyn, N.Y.

I sleep each night a little better, a little more confidently, because Lyndon Johnson is my President. For I know he lives and thinks and works to make sure that for all America, and indeed the growing body of the free world, the morning shall always come.

JACK VALENTI

CONTENTS

These quotations have been taken from the speeches, musings and digressions of Lyndon Baines Johnson. Their date and source are noted for reference. No effort has been made to rework these heroic thoughts into grammatical English.

Let workers, peasants, students, housewives and Republicans study, memorize and digest the exhortations of Chairman Johnson. Let little children add their tiny voices to public and private recitations of these joyous inspirations.

JACK SHEPHERD
CHRISTOPHER S. WREN
Translators

I. ARDUOUS STRUGGLE

Hello down there. This is your candidate, Lyndon Johnson.

> Campaigning by helicopter for U.S. Senate
> Texas, 1948

I'm not smart enough to make a President. I come from the wrong part of the country. I like the Senate job; it's the best job I've ever had. I want to stay here.

> Quoted in *Time*
> June 22, 1953

I don't remember that I have ever reached for the Presidency. My friends put me in the race in 1960.

> ABC-TV interview
> March 26, 1963

I will be President first, but we will be out campaigning when the opportunity permits, to the extent it permits.

At the same time, we will have to dedicate airports and we will have a dam here and there, and we have visitors from here and there, and we will have interviews and press conferences and we will have all of these other things that are part of the Presidency.

News conference
Washington, D.C.
September 21, 1964

Alexandria has been chosen as the first stop for one of the greatest campaigners in America, and I am very proud to announce that I am her husband.

Alexandria, Virginia
October 6, 1964

So what you do is just reach up there and get that lever and just say, "All the way with LBJ."

Your mamas and your papas and your grandpas, some of them are going to forget this. But I am depending on you young folks who are going to have to fight our wars, and who are going to have to defend this country, and who are going to get blown up if we have a nuclear holocaust—I am depending on you to have enough interest in your future and what is ahead of you to get up and prod mama and papa and make them get up early and go vote.

Airport rally
Wilmington, Delaware
October 31, 1964

I don't believe the President of the United States ought to debate with anybody.

Washington, D.C.
December 15, 1963

I try to keep as far away from partisanship and campaigning as I can.

News conference
Washington, D.C.
April 18, 1964

But I guess as long as I am here, we might as well talk a little politics.

Evansville, Indiana
October 27, 1964

II. GLORIOUS DEMOCRATIC PARTY

You Senators and reporters—you better saddle your horses and put on your spurs if you're going to keep up with Johnson on the flag, mother and corruption.

Quoted in *Time*
March 5, 1956

Food, that's *F,* and recreation, that's *R,* income is *I,* and education, that's *E,* and Social Security and Medicare and nursing homes, that's *N,* and a strong nation that will keep its promise and keep a good defense, that's *D.*

That spells out what the Democratic party stands for: Friend . . . the friend of all American families.

Wilmington, Delaware
October 13, 1966

The Democratic party has made good on its 1960 promises and has America on the march. I am proud to be a member of a party that may have turned off the lights in the White House—but had turned on the lights of hope all across the land.

$100-a-plate dinner
Atlantic City, New Jersey
May 9, 1964

I'm so glad to see so many unarmed Democrats in one room. We Democrats like to be together, and we like to fight. We start by fighting each other. That gets us ready—it says here—to take on the other party.

$250-a-plate dinner
Washington, D.C.
May 9, 1967

There is not any combination in the country that can take on Russell Long, Allen Ellender, Lyndon Johnson, and a few others if we are together.

New Orleans, Louisiana
October 9, 1964

Senator Ellender gets me to do nearly everything he wants me to do without any pilon or lagniappe. But when the going gets tough and he just really has to move heaven and earth, he will put on one of those good feeds of his and he will bring up some of this New Orleans candy that he makes, that we call pralines.

I thought he just reserved it for myself until the other day when I went over to have lunch at the White House and the table was empty, with just one plate there. I said, "Where in the world is Mrs. Johnson?" and they said, "She is up eating with Senator Ellender."

I said, "How long has she been gone?" And they said, "About fifteen minutes."

So I put on my hat and invited myself. I

went up there and I was the only man there except Allen, and he had all the pretty women in Washington up there in the room eating with him!

New Orleans, Louisiana
October 9, 1964

Nobody in this world can put on a political rally like that great executive Dick Daley of Chicago. He makes it so much fun being a Democrat that you don't see how anybody could be anything else.

Chicago, Illinois
October 30, 1964

And you don't just send Bob Kennedy to Washington when you elect him Senator. He, like the rest of us, outmarried himself, and you send one of the most effective, intelligent, and gracious persons that I have ever known—Ethel Kennedy. I think so much of her that when we had great problems in my State and we were evenly divided, the first person I asked to come to Texas, even before I asked the Democratic Presidential candidate, was Ethel Kennedy.

Rochester, New York
October 15, 1964

. . . Our message is a simple one: Vote Democratic.

Newark, New Jersey
October 7, 1966

So let's just don't talk, and let's just don't yell and let's just don't brag. Let's talk to our kinfolks and our uncles and our cousins and our aunts, and let's go do our duty November third and vote Democratic.

Baltimore, Maryland
October 24, 1964

So when you go into that ballot box, take that lever and pull it all the way down and vote the Democratic ticket straight. Don't go in there and start messing here and here and here, and get your ballot all mixed up where you don't know yourself how you voted, and they can't count, and they throw it out.

Dover, Delaware
October 31, 1964

Were you pleased with the results of the last Atlantic City convention? Well, that is wonderful. I was a little worried at first whether they made the right choice—for Miss America.

Atlantic City, New Jersey
September 22, 1964

III. UNWORTHY OTHER PARTY

I am a fellow that likes small parties, and the Republican party is about the size I like.

Washington, D.C.
April 21, 1964

Lincoln was right about not fooling all the people all of the time. But the Republicans haven't given up trying.

Newark, New Jersey
October 7, 1966

We are just sorry that one of our Democrats agreed with two Republicans. I know he was sincere and I know he thought he was doing the right thing, and men do have different opinions.

News conference
Washington, D.C.
October 3, 1964

Some of our most distinguished Americans, as well as some of my warmest friends, are Vermont Republicans.

Burlington, Vermont
September 28, 1964

I buy my cattle out here in New Mexico, the best breeds, and ship them down to Texas, and then talk about what fine cattle we raise down there. I just have to make a confession. I buy them from a fellow whose judgment about cattle is a lot better than his judgment about politics. He is Albert Mitchell, who used to be Republican national committeeman. But he sure does have fine cattle.

Albuquerque, New Mexico
October 28, 1964

I am going to always, when I am dealing with the Republicans, do like I do when I am dealing with other people in the world. I am going to keep my guard up and my hand out.

Washington, D.C.
April 21, 1964

I have learned to expect Republican criticism, and I have endured it for about thirty-two years. I get amused by it once in a while, but I don't want to change it because I think that is kind of a hallmark of their party. You get accustomed to expecting it.

News conference
Washington, D.C.
January 26, 1964

I voted for and I supported that Republican President more on his Republican program than some present members of the Republican party did. And I never at any time called it by another name. At times

I differed. On occasions I opposed but I opposed it with dignity and decency. And you never heard from the lips of a single member of the Democratic party that President Eisenhower's program was just a ten-cent model of the New Deal.

Hartford, Connecticut
September 28, 1964

The Republican party today, now, is in temporary receivership. Responsible Republicans can't do anything about it.

Bergen, New Jersey
October 14, 1964

The Republican symbol is the elephant and the elephant never forgets. The Republicans remember that they have always been elected by scaring people. Their platform this year is made up of one word. And that word is fear.

Newark, New Jersey
October 7, 1966

No, I don't have any favorite opponent. It is not my duty to select my opposition.

News conference
Washington, D.C.
February 1, 1964

You talk to Senator Goldwater about his views. I have expressed mine positively, affirmatively and completely, without reference to anybody or Senator Goldwater, but just myself. If I say I believe I loved my mother, you would say it is a jab at Senator Goldwater.

News conference
Washington, D.C.
September 5, 1964

I guess I can have a little fun on Saturday night, can't I? One of these nice fellows from Maryland that always has a good joke stood up here just now and said, "Do you know what those signs are? Now don't get upset about them."

And I said, "No, what?"

He said, "Don't you see them back there?"

I could see them, but I don't have good eyesight for a long distance. I said, "No, what do they say?"

And he said, "They say, 'Gold for the rich, water for the poor, and Johnson for President.'"

Really, I don't want you to get angry with them. Let's be charitable with everybody. Let's turn the other cheek and be nice.

Baltimore, Maryland
October 24, 1964

When the Russians sent up Sputnik I, anybody that could read and write in this country got frightened.

I immediately went to Washington and called an investigation, and we had the best military experts in the world come there and testify. While they were testifying, the Russians sent up Sputnik II, "Beep, beep, beep," around in the air.

They called for some comments from some leaders. I said we better get going, we better step up our effort. My opponent said, and this is approximately what he said, about what he said, "I am not worried about somebody putting a basketball in the air that says, 'Beep, beep, beep.' I would rather lob one into the men's room in the Kremlin."

Los Angeles, California
October 28, 1964

So it seems to me that even at the price of some reflection the Republican candidate ought to keep his lenses in his glasses, at least on the subject of nuclear warheads.

News conference
Washington, D.C.
August 15, 1964

The chairman of the Republican National Committee—I can't remember his name right now, but they chose him later to run for national office. They said, "He drives Lyndon Johnson nuts."

Newark, New Jersey
October 7, 1966

I just knew in my heart that it was not right for Dick Nixon to ever be President of this country.

Pittsburgh, Pennsylvania
October 27, 1964

IV. STATESMANSHIP AND CRISIS DIPLOMACY

Ten hours of the day, out of fourteen, I spend on the world—Latin America, European problems, Vietnam, relations with the Soviet Union. I'm gonna meet with all the ambassadors, maybe take them down to the ranch, and go for a boat ride.

Washington, D.C.
July 14, 1965

And now I want to tell you that we have a great event in store for all of you: The happy warrior, the eloquent spokesman for the Democratic Party, the new Vice President of the United States, is arriving tomorrow at noon, and in his honor and in the honor of the men and women who traveled with us in this campaign, we are going to have a barbecue out on the banks of the Pedernales.

Austin, Texas
November 4, 1964

I cannot spend the time on detailed questions, because the Prime Minister of Iceland has landed and is en route to the White House now. He is going to come in the southwest gate and I will greet him and take him into the office for a meeting. If you want to, I will take him on a little walk. I haven't had one and you can go with us.

News conference
Washington, D.C.
August 18, 1964

Shake, shake, Blanco, shake.

Introducing collie to Italian Foreign Minister Amintore Fanfani
Washington, D.C.
May 25, 1965

We shall be working hard while you are here, but there will also be time to meet some of our neighbors, to see us as we are, and to join us in a Texas barbecue.

To Chancellor Ludwig Erhard of
West Germany
Bergstrom AFB, Texas
December 28, 1963

First, I want to present Mr. Lewis Douglas, former ambassador to Great Britain.

Now, Lew, you stand up a little longer. There are some girls down here who didn't get to see you.

White House dinner
Washington, D.C.
December 7, 1964

Ambassador Goldberg, of course, is eager to come back because he's just naturally more at home in cowboy country.

News conference
LBJ Ranch, Texas
August 29, 1965

I want to get his views, and we might talk on problems over the carcass of a deer.

About Gov. Buford Ellington of Tennessee
LBJ Ranch, Texas
December 25, 1963

I want to thank all of you who served on the committee that brought us this barbecue, the fine singing, the good band, the excellent speaker that you will hear a little later, and these distinguished guests.

Stonewall, Texas
August 29, 1964

V. THE LONG MARCH TOWARD THE GREAT SOCIETY

So we tonight, assembled here, pledge ourselves to democracy's greatest tradition, the New Freedom of Wilson, the New Deal of Roosevelt, the Fair Deal of Harry S Truman, the New America and the New Frontier of John Fitzgerald Kennedy, and after Tuesday, November third, the Great Society of Lyndon Johnson and Hubert Humphrey.

Chicago, Illinois
October 30, 1964

I think you can say about the Great Society—it sure is crowded.

Inaugural Ball
Washington, D.C.
January 20, 1965

But we're only at the beginning of the road to the Great Society. Ahead now is a summit where freedom from the wants of the body can help fulfill the needs of the spirit.

State of the Union message
Washington, D.C.
January 4, 1965

So I ask you tonight to join me and march along the road to the future, the road that leads to the Great Society, where no child will go unfed and no youngster will go unschooled; where every child has a good teacher and every teacher has good pay, and both have good classrooms; where every human being has dignity and every worker has a job; where education is blind to color and employment is unaware of race; where decency prevails and courage abounds.

New York, New York
May 28, 1964

So as we go down the long, winding, uphill trail of a greater society, a better America, a place where every family has a roof over its head, where every child has an opportunity for an education, where there is a rug on the floor and a picture on the wall and a little music in the house—let's stand up behind that leadership of your country which says: Tomorrow will be better than yesterday!

Cleveland, Ohio
June 17, 1964

Will you leave the future a society where lawns are clipped and the countryside cluttered, where store buildings are new and school buildings are old; a society of private satisfaction for some in the midst of public squalor for all? Or will you join to build the Great Society?

Austin, Texas
May 30, 1964

. . . The Great Society is not a safe harbor, a resting place, a final objective, a finished work. It is a challenge constantly renewed, beckoning us toward a destiny where the meaning of our lives matches the marvelous products of our labor.

Ann Arbor, Michigan
May 22, 1964

I have in mind for this country a Great Society, where every boy and girl has a right to all the education they can take; where every man and his wife have a right to hope for and an expectancy to get a home that they can call their own; where every man and woman who is willing to work can work; where we work fewer hours per day and fewer days per week; and we have a beautiful countryside—someday I hope to get rid of all these old secondhand autos out on the highway—to have a beautiful countryside with seashores and parks where the kiddies can go and play and enjoy the land of their fathers.

Oh, what I perceive for this nation in the year 2000 is so exciting to me that I just hope the doctors hurry up and get busy and let me live that long.

Cleveland, Ohio
October 8, 1964

And if the young leadership of our country supports us over the long hard pull that lies ahead, if you can endure the tensions, if you can understand that the air is going to be rough and the road is going to be bumpy, and you can, in the words of your own creed, help us unlock earth's great treasure, human personality, then the cussers and the doubters will be relegated to the rear. And the doers and the builders will take up the front line.

Baltimore, Maryland
June 27, 1967

We have made a major and significant beginning to throttle want and elevate hope.

Austin, Texas
January 17, 1965

Oh, what you have done to lead the way in the field of education is an inspiration to all of us who come here. So keep up your leadership. Go on your forward march in this great work until the day comes when all have homes, when all children are taught all they can absorb, when we have recreation to take care of our leisure time, and when brother loves brother and neighbor embraces neighbor.

Sacramento, California
September 17, 1964

I do not believe that the Great Society is the ordered, changeless and sterile battalion of the ants.

Washington, D.C.
January 20, 1965

Now, I want to participate in helping you to dedicate your Parade of Progress by pushing the button to start the mall fountains.

By telephone to Cleveland, Ohio
Atlantic City, New Jersey
August 28, 1964

VI. FRUGALITY AND THRIFT

We are going to put "thrift" back in the dictionary.

Washington, D.C.
December 4, 1964

Soft budgets do not build a strong America. Flabby fiscal practices are enemies not only of our muscle and our might; they are enemies of mental capabilities and moral concepts.

Washington, D.C.
July 21, 1964

Someone told me that the light bill in the White House ran several thousand dollars a month. I challenged Mr. [Jack] Valenti over there and my maid this morning when

I left to turn out all those lights in those chandeliers when there is no one in the house. Mrs. Johnson had gone to New York and I was the only one there, and I didn't require that much light.

I don't know how much we saved today. I want a bill for the last three months to see if we are making any headway. And see that that goes down to every government building. A stitch in time saves nine. You don't accumulate anything unless you save the small amounts.

To Bureau of Budget officials
Washington, D.C.
January 20, 1964

In trying to keep unnecessary expenditures down I believe the President ought to be as unsatisfied as a little boy's appetite.

White House luncheon
Washington, D.C.
October 6, 1964

I don't believe that we are going to make the Treasury over by cutting out a few automobiles or turning out a few lights. But I do think it is a good example when you walk through the corridor and you see the closets where lights burn all day and all night just because someone didn't turn them off.

National TV and radio interview
March 15, 1964

We use more power to burn fewer lights than any other house in the land.

Washington, D.C.
May 20, 1964

I want to spend everything that is necessary to spend to keep moving our country forward progressively. In order to do that, I don't want to waste a dime.

News conference
Washington, D.C.
December 7, 1963

With Secretary McNamara present here today, I don't want to set a bad precedent on cost reduction, so Lady Bird and I are trying to finish this party before we have to turn on the lights.

White House military reception
on the lawn
Washington, D.C.
May 26, 1965

I think I should tell you that the stories they write about the White House being in the dark are greatly exaggerated. There is some truth in the statement that Lynda and Luci do study by kerosene lamps occasionally, but it is on the ranch and not in Washington. But when the sun comes up, we always open the curtains.

Washington, D.C.
March 4, 1964

As we say on the farm, "Maybe we ought to try to get by with some baling wire, patch things up," to get by during this particular period when there is such pressure on our economy.

News conference
Washington, D.C.
September 22, 1966

Using pony express, copies of Lincoln's address were delivered from Washington to California in seven days and seventeen hours, by seventy-five ponies, at a cost of $5 per one-half ounce.

Today, for only 5¢ we can send three ounces of Presidential addresses across the country—at about the same rate of speed.

Washington, D.C.
February 19, 1965

If we keep getting bills down here like the education bill and the pollution bill, I am going to have to take new bids on pens to see if we cannot increase the budget by getting cheaper pens!

Washington, D.C.
December 17, 1963

I wanted to call collect, but Lady Bird wouldn't let me. And then I only have change for three minutes.

Birthday call to Harry Truman
Washington, D.C.
May 6, 1964

If any of you are the faintest bit interested you can go over there and see the loading pens. That's where the cattle go out and the money comes in.

LBJ Ranch, Texas
December 25, 1963

We are going in shortly to the White House, so you can pick up your candles in a box over there.

Washington, D.C.
April 17, 1964

VII. ENLIGHTENED BROTHERHOOD

No part of the above described premises shall ever be conveyed or in any way transferred, demised, leased or rented to any person or persons of African descent; provided that this clause shall not prevent the employment of such persons as domestic servants and providing customary accommodations for them.

> Anti-Negro covenant inserted in deed for Austin, Texas, property sold by Lyndon B. Johnson in 1945

This civil rights program about which you have heard so much is a farce and a sham—an effort to set up a police state in the guise of liberty. I am opposed to that program. I fought it in Congress. It is the province of the state to run its own elections. I am opposed to the anti-lynching bill because the Federal Government has no more business enacting a law against one kind of murder than another. I am against the FEPC because if a man can tell you whom you must hire, he can tell you whom you cannot employ. I have met this head-on.

Austin, Texas
May 22, 1948

Such a law [FEPC legislation] would necessitate a system of Federal police officers such as we have never before seen. It would require the policing of every business institution, every transaction made between an employer and employee, and virtually every hour of an employer's and employee's association while at work.

U.S. Senate speech, March 9, 1949

I am naturally concerned that you think I have made concessions with respect to the so-called civil rights issue. I assure you that I feel the way I have always felt. That is that I am firmly opposed to forced integration and I firmly believe that the doctrine of states' rights should be maintained.

Form letter to constituent
February 18, 1957

In 1960, immediately after the election, President Kennedy asked me to devote some time to this work and no assignment that I received from him was ever closer to my heart or my interests.

The ideal of equal opportunity, I believe, is the bedrock ideal of our society and of our system. I am grateful for the opportunity I had to work for that ideal's greater realization.

Washington, D.C.
July 7, 1964

Justice requires us to remember—when any citizen denies his fellow, saying, "His color is not mine" or "His beliefs are strange and different"—in that moment he betrays America, though his forebears created this nation.

Washington, D.C.
January 20, 1965

And we shall overcome.

Washington, D.C.
March 15, 1965

VIII. PASSIONS OF PERSUASION

I'm a compromiser and a maneuverer. I try to get *something.* That's the way our system works. . . .

Quoted in the *New York Times*
Section IV
December 8, 1963

I am a child of the Congress. For more than thirty years the Hill was my home, and I am here tonight among those that I know, and that I respect and that I love.

Washington, D.C.
June 24, 1965

Congress has done a good job. They are doing a good job. Some folks play politics. They give out statements. I see on the ticker about three or four handouts a day. They are usually some new press man who has been hired, or a fellow who thinks he is being paid by the column, like a stringer. He gives out these handouts and provokes fights. He puts a little twist on it. But the Congress is doing a good job, and the people know it.

News conference
Washington, D.C.
March 22, 1966

Fooling the people has become the name of the game for a good many Republicans in Congress. They vote one way on the motion to recommit a bill to committee and then the opposite way on the final passage of the bill. They know that the motion to recommit a bill is the motion to kill a bill—a motion to put a dagger in its heart.

Newark, New Jersey
October 7, 1966

On January fourth we laid the program down. And then we fogged them in, the messages, one by one. You know, Congress can't take too many at once. If you take a jigger of bourbon at a time you can drink a long time. But if you drink a pint all at once, it'll come up on you.

We don't twist arms. Most of that comes from people who are not informed. At our meetings with the Congressional leaders the report is from them to us. We don't tell them what to do.

Washington, D.C.
July 14, 1965

You writers like to write about Lyndon Johnson's Black Magic and so on; and about Lyndon Johnson's scheming and maneuvering and manipulating. But it's not like that at all. Of course, when we get the football in our hands, we don't just sit back with it—when we don't hit the line, we throw a forward pass. . . . People don't understand one thing about me, that is that the one thing I want to do is my job. Some are always writing that I'm a back-room operator. They say I'm sensitive. How would you like your little daughter to read that you are a "backroom operator," a "wire-puller" or a "clever man"?

Quoted in *Lyndon B. Johnson: Man and President,* 1963

IX. WAR AND PEACE

The Secretary of Defense emphasizes that the current population boom offers an unprecedented challenge to our armed services to try to strengthen their voluntary recruitment program.

News conference
Washington, D.C.
October 3, 1964

I hate war. And if the day ever comes when my vote must be cast to send your boy to the trenches, that day Lyndon Johnson will leave his Senate seat to go with him.

Unsuccessful campaign for U.S. Senate
Texas, 1941

When they lead your boy down to that railroad station to send him into boot camp and put a khaki uniform on him to send him some place where he may never return, they don't ask you whether you are a Republican or a Democrat. They send you there to defend that flag, and you go.

Pittsburgh, Pennsylvania
October 27, 1964

When we line them up at the reception centers to fit them for their uniforms, we don't say, "What is your church? What is your political affiliation? What section of the country do you live in and who was your grandpa?" We say, "Give him size 42." . . .

Baltimore, Maryland
October 1, 1964

As your President I deal every day with the problems that affect your freedom and affect the peace of the world. Those problems may be remote from this peaceful site out here this afternoon. Not many of you get waked up in the night about Cyprus, or Zanzibar, or Vietnam. But I never send a reconnaisance mission out about 11 o'clock in our planes with our boys guiding them to take a look at what is developing, and realize they have to be back at 3:30 in the morning, but what promptly at 3:25 I wake up without an alarm clock, because I want to be sure my boys get back.

Eufaula, Oklahoma
September 25, 1964

We had a little problem right after I came in down at Guantanamo. Mr. Castro—that bearded fellow—came out there one morning and decided to cut our water off, and wouldn't let our servicemen have water at the base. We were contracting with him to buy water. And then everything went up. We have hotheads everywhere, you know, and smart alecks, and folks that have ideas.

So they immediately started giving suggestions, and we got a lot of them. But we decided that we ought to move one of our plants from California and make our own water and quit paying Mr. Castro for it, let him take his outfit and go on home.

Wilmington, Delaware
October 31, 1964

. . . I had some military experts, some generals here and there, that hollered at me right loudly and said, "Please send in the Marines immediately."

I didn't see any reason to send in the Marines to cut the water off. I just sent in one admiral to turn it off and kept the Marines at home. I didn't start any war, although I would like very much to see the free people of Cuba be able to govern themselves without the dictations of Mr. Castro.

Stonewall, Texas
August 29, 1964

I do not genuinely believe that there's any single person anywhere in the world that wants peace as much as I want it.

Chicago, Illinois
May 17, 1966

The type of gas that is a standard item in the South Vietnamese military forces —anti-riot item—can be purchased by any individual from open stocks in this country just like you order something out of a Sears and Roebuck catalogue.

I don't mean Sears and Roebuck's handling any gas, but it's the same—a catalogue almost that large—any of you can order it. If you felt that I was endangering your life and your family, you could use it on me right now in this room and it would bring some tears and it would nauseate me for—some of them three minutes and some five minutes, sometimes up to an hour. It would not kill me or kill you.

News conference
Washington, D.C.
April 1, 1965

. . . Just because we have a button here that will put off a blast over yonder is no reason you want to put that thumb on that button.

Nashville, Tennessee
October 9, 1964

I want the mothers who must supply the boys, and I want the boys who must die in the wars, to know that no impulsive act of mine, no heat of emotion, is ever going to cause me to do a rash, dangerous, adventurous thing that might wipe out 300 million Americans.

Memphis, Tennessee
October 24, 1964

As long as I am your President, I am not going to rattle our rockets, I am not going to bluff with our bombs. I am going to keep our guard up at all times and our hand out.

But I am going to be willing to go anywhere, see anyone, talk anytime to try to bring peace to this world so these mothers will not have to give up their boys and have them wiped out in a nuclear holocaust.

Casper, Wyoming
October 12, 1964

I sat in the Cabinet Room for thirty-seven meetings during the Cuban missile crisis. I saw Mr. Khrushchev bring his missiles into Cuba, 90 miles from our shores and point them in our direction. I saw Mr. Kennedy bring in all the men with the stars on their shoulders and the gold braid on their uniforms. I saw the great diplomat, the Secretary of State, the Rhodes scholar, come in and make his recommendations.

I never knew a single morning when I left home that I would see my wife and daughters again that night.

Wichita, Kansas
October 29, 1964

I never left home a single day during those thirty-eight sessions that I knew for sure I would see my wife and daughters again that night.

. . . Our bombers were in the skies and our bomb bays were ready to be opened. They were loaded. Our ships were in their proper places. Our men had their proper instructions. But when the time finally came, the good Lord somehow or other decreed that there would not be a nuclear holocaust that would wipe out the lives of 300 million people, 100 million right here in our own land.

Pittsburgh, Pennsylvania
October 27, 1964

Yes, we are a mighty nation. We know it and they know it. We covet no one's territory. We seek to dominate no people. We know it and they know it. That is why you gain nothing from bravado; that is why you gain nothing from rattling your rockets and bluffing with your bombs. That is why you get nowhere by saying you'll lob one into the men's room in the Kremlin.

Detroit, Michigan
October 30, 1964

So peace—peace, that simple little five-letter word—is the most important word in the English language to us at this time and it occupies more of our attention than any other word or any other subject.

News conference
Washington, D.C.
August 25, 1965

So you are going to have to select the man whose thumb will be close to that button. You are going to have to select the man who will answer that telephone, that "hot line" from Moscow, when that bell starts jingling, ting-a-ling-a-ling, and they say,

"Moscow is calling." You are going to have to select the President, and you have only one President.

Wilmington, Delaware
October 31, 1964

You send a message just like you send a cable. There is no voice involved. The "hot line" was something dramatic, I guess. We just write our message, giving our views, and say, "Here is how we feel about it." They come back with the same message. You take it and read it as you would any other message.

News conference
Washington, D.C.
June 13, 1967

So I would say that the reports from the front are good. We must not be too optimistic and we must not exaggerate what is taking place. But I get about one hundred letters a week from them, and I would say they are my greatest source of strength. If I get real depressed when I read how everything has gone bad here, I just ask for the letters from Vietnam so I can cheer up.

News conference
Washington, D.C.
March 22, 1966

X. MORE WAR AND PEACE

Our one desire—our one determination—is that the people of southeast Asia be left in peace to work out their own destinies in their own way.

Washington, D.C.
August 10, 1964

Some others are eager to enlarge the conflict. They call upon us to supply American boys to do the job that Asian boys should do. They ask us to take reckless action which might risk the lives of millions and engulf much of Asia and certainly threaten the peace of the entire world. Moreover, such action would offer no solution at all to the real problem of Vietnam.

New York, New York
August 12, 1964

I have had advice to load our planes with bombs and to drop them on certain areas that I think would enlarge the war and escalate the war, and result in our committing a good many American boys to fighting a war that I think ought to be fought by the boys of Asia to help protect their own land.

Stonewall, Texas
August 29, 1964

There are those that say you ought to go north and drop bombs, to try to wipe out the supply lines, and they think that would escalate the war. We don't want our American boys to do the fighting for Asian boys. We don't want to get involved in a nation with 700 million people and get tied down in a land war in Asia.

Eufaula, Oklahoma
September 25, 1964

As far as I am concerned, I want to be very cautious and careful, and use it only as a last resort, when I start dropping bombs around that are likely to involve American boys in a war in Asia with 700 million Chinese.

So just for the moment I have not thought that we were ready for American boys to do the fighting for Asian boys. What I have been trying to do, with the situation that I found, was to get the boys in Vietnam to do their own fighting with our advice and with our equipment. That is the course we are following. So we are not going north and drop bombs at this stage of the game, and we are not going south and run out and leave it for the Communists to take over.

Manchester, New Hampshire
September 28, 1964

In Asia we face an ambitious and aggressive China, but we have the will and we have the strength to help our Asian friends resist that ambition. Sometimes our folks get a little impatient. Sometimes they rattle their rockets some, and they bluff about their bombs. But we are not about to send American boys nine or ten thousand miles away from home to do what Asian boys ought to be doing for themselves.

Akron, Ohio
October 21, 1964

The drumbeat of history is quickening. . . . We have had nine governments alone in Vietnam since I became President.

Washington, D.C.
February 17, 1965

Our one desire and our one determination is that the people of southeast Asia be left in peace to work out their own destinies in their own ways.

News conference
Washington, D.C.
March 13, 1965

In recent months attacks on South Vietnam were stepped up. Thus, it became necessary for us to increase our response and to make attacks by air. This is not a change of purpose. It is a change in what we believe that purpose requires.

Baltimore, Maryland
April 7, 1965

I regret the necessities of war have compelled us to bomb North Vietnam. We have carefully limited those raids. They have been directed at radar stations, bridges and ammunition dumps, not at population centers. They have been directed at concrete and steel, and not human life.

. . . The people of South Vietnam and the Americans who share their struggle suffer because they are attacked, not because they are attackers.

. . . And let this also be clear: Until [their] independence is guaranteed there is no human power capable of forcing us from Vietnam.

LBJ Ranch, Texas
April 17, 1965

I have today ordered to Vietnam the Air-mobile Division and certain other forces which will raise our fighting strength from 75,000 to 125,000 men almost immediately. Additional forces will be needed later, and they will be sent as requested.

This will make it necessary to increase our active fighting forces by raising the monthly draft call from 17,000 over a period of time to 35,000 per month, and for us to step up our campaign for voluntary enlistments.

News conference
Washington, D.C.
July 28, 1965

Since Christmas your Government has labored again, with imagination and endurance, to remove any barrier to peaceful settlement. For twenty days now we and our Vietnamese allies have dropped no bombs in North Vietnam.

State of the Union message
Washington, D.C.
January 12, 1966

I didn't get us into Vietnam. I didn't ring up out there and say, "I want some trouble." I was out there in '61, one of the first things that I did. President Kennedy sent me out there when we were worried about the stability of the government there. We can't pick other people's governments. We have enough trouble picking our own.

Louisville, Kentucky
October 9, 1964

Now I knew nothing about the gas. No one told me that the South Vietnamese were going to use any tear gas any more than they told me that they were going to shoot this fellow that dropped the bomb, left the bomb in his car in front of our embassy, but there is no reason why they should.

If the United States military forces were going to use poisonous gas, of course the Commander in Chief would know about it. . . .

News conference
Washington, D.C.
April 1, 1965

Your daddy may go down in history as having started World War III.

To Luci
Quoted in the *Washington Post*
May 12, 1967

XI. THE FAITHFUL PRESS

The press helps me. The press is one of the best servants I have.

Washington, D.C.
July 14, 1965

I would say we all ought to be commended for our good spirits and jolly frame of mind. I appreciate the good humor you are all in. I don't know how to account for it.

News conference
Washington, D.C.
March 22, 1966

I think that there are very few Presidents in the history of this country that have had more support of more publishers and more magazines than the present President.

News conference
Washington, D.C.
July 13, 1965

I have seen thirty or forty reporters who have asked to come in on special things that they wanted to do. Some of them wanted to write about Cousin Oriole. Some of them want to write about what I think about my wife. Some of them want to tell their editor that they saw me and here is what they think will happen in the wild blue yonder. I try to see all of them I can with my schedule and I am very happy with them. I never enjoy anything more than polite, courteous, fair, judicious reporters, and I think all of you qualify.

News conference
Washington, D.C.
January 25, 1964

One of the most noted leaders of this country said to me the other day that I must constantly be aware when I am talking to you that everything about our Government is not bad, and I am not necessarily on trial, and we are not criminals here to have to argue and reply on every course of action, and that we need not explain any more of the details than is necessary to see the public has a reasonable knowledge.

To White House correspondents
Washington, D.C.
August 9, 1965

As I told you in the beginning, I always want to remain accessible. I hope the press will never be critical of me for being over-accessible.

News conference
Washington, D.C.
May 6, 1964

. . . Today marks the 39th on-the-record press conference that I have held, 18 off-the-record, or a total of 57. I have had 18 press conferences with adequate advance notice, 16 covered by radio and television. . . . In addition to these 56 formal meetings I have had 9 informal, lengthy walks with the White House press corps. . . . We had 173 airplane flights with pools. . . . I have had additional visits from 374 accredited press representatives at their request; in addition, 64 who requested meetings as bureau chiefs, plus 200 telephone discussions that I have responded to.

News conference
LBJ Ranch, Texas
March 20, 1965

[Press conferences] are a kind of prearranged show where some reporters get to stand up and be on TV.

Quoted in *Newsweek*
February 15, 1965

You may not be able to tell it by just looking at them, but I want to give my personal testimony in behalf of the newspapermen and newspaperwomen that they are doing very well in our own White House physical fitness training program on our daily walks. We have had very few casualties—we have lost one or two high heels, and one or two dropouts, but generally speaking, the marks are high. Give me a little more time, and both the press and, I hope, the President will be in better shape. . . . I want to say thank you very much, and we will have our 114th walk a little later in the day.

Washington, D.C.
May 3, 1965

You're always asking me when I'm coming and like to know when I'm going. I don't know. You ask George Reedy every hour on the hour. I want a couple of days' rest.

To reporters
Fredericksburg, Texas
August 30, 1964

I just suggested that it was rather difficult for a fellow to take a glass of water at the White House, or even go out to the hydrant and get a drink, without it being adequately publicized. I can't even visit with my dogs without a lot of publicity.

News conference
Washington, D.C.
July 24, 1964

We are going over and get a little hors d'oeuvre and sandwich in a moment, and then we are going to Atlantic City. Those who want to go, talk to George, and if we have room in our plane I will be glad to have you go with us under the regular rules that you follow. . . .

[Q. What time do you plan to take off for Atlantic City?]

After we get an hors d'oeuvre and get some planes, and get me there in time for 9:15. If we work it out, we will go in Air Force One. If there are too many, I will go in the Jet Star and you can go in a second plane, but you will have to reimburse the Air Force. Does anyone know how many we can haul in Air Force One? See if we can't have a follow-up plane. How many want to go? Hold up those hands and somebody count them.

News conference
Washington, D.C.
August 26, 1964

I enjoy seeing the press. I learn much from reporters. In the White House press corps alone, there are at least half a dozen experts already on animal husbandry.

Washington, D.C.
May 11, 1964

Now if the photographers will leave my dog alone, I will go on and finish this speech. They will be blaming me for that before it is over, and saying I am talking too loud or too low, but I think that is a UP photographer. The AP photographer is better trained. I mean they have specialized in dogs over a longer period of time.

Washington, D.C.
May 16, 1964

I can assure you that at times, especially after I read the newspapers, I have strong urges to be a writer. In fact, if I may turn the tables, I sometimes think some of my friends in the press need some new writers.

Washington, D.C.
April 30, 1964

I saw the story and I would say that probably represents a highly aggressive reporter who met a man who wanted to appear smart.

News conference
LBJ Ranch, Texas
January 16, 1965

I haven't read the Paris magazines.

News conference
LBJ Ranch, Texas
July 5, 1966

. . . During the period that we have had the most hectic, distressing moments here in Washington, the poll has gone up 6 per cent out in the country, so I sometimes think maybe it just may be July in the Nation's Capital.

News conference
Washington, D.C.
July 13, 1965

We, of course, would like for every poll to be of our own liking. And we'd like to feel that all of them are accurate. We have had a dozen polls, I guess, in the last week. You don't read about the favorable ones, so I've observed.

News conference
LBJ Ranch, Texas
July 5, 1966

We don't base our actions on the Gallup Poll.

News conference
Washington, D.C.
July 31, 1967

. . . I am proud to say that despite whatever you read, really some of my best friends are newspapermen and women.

Washington, D.C.
May 18, 1965

I think that those of us who sit here in Washington and watch what three networks put on the air and what three men decide—you can observe from Vietnam and all the international incidents, read six or seven columnists, two or three or four newspapers. Sometimes we don't get it firsthand and sometimes there's a little personal equation that gets into it and sometimes personal opinions are substituted for facts, and I think it's good to get out and see the people and talk to 'em and I am convinced that the complainers in this country and the critics in this country and the prophets of doom in this country and the fear artists in this country are very, very much in the minority.

News conference
Washington, D.C.
October 13, 1966

Somebody ought to do an article on *you,* on your damn profession, your First Amendment.

To reporters
Washington, D.C.
July 14, 1965

XII. HUMILITY AND SELF-CRITICISM

XIII. BENIGN DESPOTISM

I have the ablest staff that ever served any President in my memory. There's not a playboy among them. They aren't sitting around . . . drinking whiskey at 11 o'clock at night. They aren't walking around with their zippers unbuttoned.

Washington, D.C.
July 14, 1965

I want people with compassion, and people who feel, and people who care around me, just as much as I want people who think.

Washington, D.C.
August 13, 1964

And a very few people I have called on have not been willing to put their shoulder to the wheel and help me.

News conference
Washington, D.C.
April 16, 1964

Nine out of ten Government employees do a full day's work for a day's pay, but I want that tenth man to measure up also.

Washington, D.C.
December 11, 1963

. . . This administration is not running a stag party.

Washington, D.C.
March 4, 1964

I spend a good deal of my day trying to find the . . . unheard of McNamaras that may be back under that table. If any of you feel like you can qualify, call up, I want to see you.

Washington, D.C.
February 25, 1965

I don't believe in harassing people; I believe in encouraging them. I don't believe in hating people; I believe in loving them. I am not filled with fear; I am filled with faith. I am not going around grouchy always doubting that it will work.

Los Angeles, California
October 28, 1964

If you ever keep Hubert waiting again, I'll kick your ass down that hall.

Quoted in *Esquire*
August, 1967

I've told Bob McNamara if anybody calls him and says he speaks for me, let me have the name of that man right away and I'll fire him. If Dean Rusk doesn't know how to run the State Department better than we do, then we ought to have somebody else.

To reporters
Washington, D.C.
July 14, 1965

There is a saying among some people to never spend your time on a colonel if there is a general in the vicinity. And my beloved friend and distinguished Vice President-elect, Senator Hubert Humphrey, I observe, has a rule, "Never sit by a man, if there is a lady in the room." Stand up, Hubert. I want to introduce you.

Washington, D.C.
December 1, 1964

He [Jack Valenti] was late to work this morning for the first time. He got in after the sun had been up and had to go pull the curtain, with the sun shining in my eyes. He is usually there early.

News conference
Washington, D.C.
September 5, 1964

I ran out of lead pencils last night in my night reading about 2 o'clock. I wondered why they didn't sharpen some that were there. They had all broken off. But there was nobody to criticize so I had to get up and go to my coat pocket and get a new pencil.

News conference
Washington, D.C.
April 22, 1966

Get this cleaned up right away or else I'll come back tonight and do it myself.

To White House secretary with messy desk
Washington, D.C.
May 17, 1964

Kilduff, I hope your mind isn't as cluttered as your desk.

To Malcolm Kilduff
Quoted in *The Wall Street Journal*
July 6, 1965

Kilduff, I hope your brain isn't as empty as your desk.

To Malcolm Kilduff a few days later
Quoted in *The Wall Street Journal*
July 6, 1965

Now, there's what I call neatness. George [Reedy] deserves a medal, his desk is so neat.

Washington, D.C.
May 17, 1964

If you ever follow dogs, you like to hear them yelp.

Washington, D.C.
April 28, 1964

The yelp is not a sound of pain. It's a sound of joy.

Washington, D.C.
May 2, 1964

You never want to give a man a present when he's feeling good. You want to do it when he's down.

Quoted in *Esquire*
August, 1967

Little Luci has been in 22 states and she came back the other day and said, "Daddy,

I have been in the Dakotas and Nebraska this weekend and I haven't had a single free weekend since last May. Do you think that is right for a seventeen-year-old?" Well, she is going to have a free weekend, thank the Lord, if the good Lord is willing and the creeks don't rise, this weekend.

Austin, Texas
November 2, 1964

Few Presidents have been so fortunate as I have been in the quality, intelligence, dedication and loyalty of those who served the country and served me in the Cabinet and in the White House. I think all of you know my gratitude is great.

Over the past year, several have departed —Ted Sorensen, Arthur Schlesinger, Brooks Hays and our new Ambassador to Chile, Ralph Dungan.

Today I am respecting the personal wishes of several others by regretfully and reluctantly announcing these further resignations:

Kenneth O'Donnell, Myer Feldman, Dave Powers, and a lady who is a dear and cherished friend of the Johnson family, Dr. Janet Travell.

News conference
LBJ Ranch, Texas
January 16, 1965

XIV. SINCERITY

Public confidence in the elective process is the foundation of public confidence in government. There is no higher duty of a democratic government than to insure that confidence.

Washington, D.C.
May 27, 1966

We cannot tolerate conflicts of interest or favoritism—or even conduct which gives the appearance that such actions are occurring—and it is our intention to see that this does not take place in the Federal Government.

Washington, D.C.
May 9, 1965

There is a question also which has been raised about a gift of a stereo set that an employee of mine made to me and Mrs. Johnson. That happened some two years later, some five years ago. The [Bobby] Baker family gave us a stereo set. We used it for a period and we had exchanged gifts before. He was an employee of the public and had no business pending before me and was asking for nothing and, so far as I knew, expected nothing in return any more than I did when I had presented him with gifts.

News conference
Washington, D.C.
January 23, 1964

I have said before that shortly after I entered office, that I have no interest in television anyplace. The interest that Mrs. Johnson held and my family held had been placed in trusteeship and any statements in connection with the operation of those interests would have to come from the trustees. I am unfamiliar with it, I am not keeping up with it, I am not concerned about it.

News conference
Washington, D.C.
April 11, 1964

Well, first, I don't have any interest in Government-regulated industries of any kind and never have had. I own no stocks. I own a little ranch land, something in excess of 2,000 acres. The Commission [FCC] has made no requests of me or of my family for anything. We are perfectly willing to comply, I am sure the trustees would be, with any request that they did make. There is not anything that we have to secrete in any manner, shape or form.

Mrs. Johnson inherited some property, invested that property in the profession of her choice, and worked at it with pleasure and satisfaction until I forced her to leave it when I assumed the Presidency. As you know, and I want all to know, all of that stock has been placed in trust, as has been the practice with other Presidents, and although I own none of it, Mrs. Johnson has placed it in trust, an irrevocable trust that the property can be disposed of, it can be leased, it can be sold at any time.

Any of those decisions would still require the action of the Commission. Even if you tried to sell it, you would have to have their approval. But I see no conflict in any way. She participates in no decisions the company makes. It is entirely with the trustees. In any event, if she did participate, the President wouldn't have anything to do with it.

News conference
Washington, D.C.
April 16, 1964

I have had no information about any dinners held for anyone to obtain funds for personal use, none that I have ever attended that I knew were being held for that purpose. I always understood that they were having an appreciation dinner or testimonial dinner but I didn't know that it was for personal, or political, or local campaign or national.

News conference
Washington, D.C.
April 22, 1966

I am unaware that I have ever driven past 70.

News conference
Washington, D.C.
April 4, 1964

Now some people say I talk out of both sides of my mouth.

Washington, D.C.
April 27, 1964

XV. ADULATION OF FRIENDS

I know I should refer to him formally as my secretary to the majority, but my tongue, even as my heart, says "Bobby" instead. His quick intelligence, his tremendous fund of knowledge about the Senate—which is appalling in one so young—has kept the machinery on this side of the aisle working with smooth precision. Always present, always alert, and more than anything else, always understanding and persuasive with his wise counsel. I say to all of you here tonight that here, indeed, is a young man of rare and real promise.

Speech on Senate floor
Washington, D.C.
July 27, 1956

He [Bobby Baker] is a man who truly serves his country, and I consider him one of my most trusted, most loyal, and most competent friends.

Speech on Senate floor
August 30, 1957

. . . There have been few times in my life that I have ever seen a young man who combined so much wisdom and maturity with such youthful vigor and enthusiasm as Bobby Baker. . . . He is a young man who has already gone very far and who is going much farther. I believe he will reach much greater heights.

Speech on Senate floor
Washington, D.C.
August 23, 1958

Baker is my strong right arm, the last man I see at night, the first one I see in the morning.

Rocky Bottom, South Carolina
1960 campaign

Well, without agreeing with your assumptions about why the investigation or who it is aimed at I would say that one of the finest committees in the Senate made up of members of both parties have been conducting this investigation of an employee of theirs—no protégé of anyone; he was there before I came to the Senate for ten years, doing a job substantially the same as he is doing now.

National TV and radio interview
March 5, 1964

XVI. MESSIANIC INFALLIBILITY

I want to thank you for that wonderful introduction. I think it was the best introduction I have ever had in my political life, except one. One time down in Texas the fellow that was supposed to show up didn't get there and I had to introduce myself.

East Chicago, Indiana
October 8, 1964

Every night when I go to bed I ask myself: "What did we do today that we can point to for generations to come, to say that we laid the foundation for a better and more peaceful and more prosperous world?"

Washington, D.C.
April 21, 1964

Every night before I turn out the lights to sleep I ask myself this question: "Have I done everything that I can do to unite this country? Have I done everything I can to help unite the world, to try to bring peace and hope to all the peoples of the world? Have I done enough?"

Baltimore, Maryland
April 7, 1965

I remember when I first came to Washington thirty-two years ago. The people who sent me to Congress were poor people. Many were hungry. But I soon saw they were only a few of the victims of a stricken land. Their recovery would only come as the entire nation recovered and grew strong.

I watched, and sometimes I helped a little, as America forged in the bitterness of common disaster a new partnership between government and business and farmers and workers.

National TV and radio address
Washington, D.C.
November 2, 1964

I will never feel that I have done justice to my high office until every section of this country is linked, in single purpose and joined devotion, to bring an end to injustice, to bring an end to poverty, and to bring an end to the threat of conflict among nations.

Atlanta, Georgia
May 8, 1964

And now, whenever I feel that I've done a good day's work, whenever I feel that I've really accomplished something, I look at that desk and then I go back to work, because I know I've only begun.

New York, New York
October 31, 1964

. . . I am directing the Federal departments and agencies to reduce their injury frequency 30 per cent by 1970.

Washington, D.C.
February 16, 1965

. . . We face towering tests of our imagination and our ingenuity, towering tests of our leadership and our labor.

New York, New York
June 6, 1964

If we succeed, think how wonderful the year 2000 will be. And it is already so exciting to me that I am just hoping that my heart and stroke and cancer committee can come up with some good results that will insure that all of us can live beyond a hundred so we can participate in that glorious day when all the fruits of our labors and our imaginations today are a reality.

Washington, D.C.
October 2, 1964

Yeah, I was interrupted by applause eighty times.

After State of the Union message
Washington, D.C.
January 8, 1964

XVII. THE HAPPY MASSES

Now you folks come on and be happy, come on and be happy.

St. Louis, Missouri
October 21, 1964

Yes, all day I have seen your smiling faces. All day I have looked into your happy countenances. All day I have seen the family life, the mothers and the children of America here in the heartland of the great state of Illinois. And those voices sound powerful to me. They sound clear. They sound free.

And when I return to the White House, and the policemen turn the keys on those locks on those big black gates, and I get to those few acres that are back of our house, it is going to be folks like you that sustain me in my labors and in my thoughts. It is going to be prayers like yours that give us inspiration and hope and leadership and make it possible for us some way, somehow, to achieve peace on earth.

Peoria, Illinois
October 7, 1964

You don't know how much better it makes me feel to look into the faces of people that look like they just stuck in their thumb and pulled out a plum, instead of looking at someone that looks like he had a teaspoon full of vinegar.

Butte, Montana
October 12, 1964

But he is the greatest producer in all the world—the American workingman. He doesn't ask much either. He wants a little vacation. He would like to have a little sick leave, he hopes he has a little medical care, he has some things that he wants, he wants a rug on the floor, and a picture on the wall, and a little music in the house. He wants a church that he can worship in according to the dictates of his own conscience. He wants a school that he can send his children to and he hopes they get better education then he got. He doesn't ask for the world with a fence around it.

Oklahoma City, Oklahoma
September 25, 1964

. . . There is the worker who gets to work at eight and works to five and he has twenty-seven seconds to put the number of rivets in that car or that plane that he needs to. If he doesn't get them in in the twenty-seven seconds he goes to twenty-eight. That car or that plane moves on down the line and it doesn't have the rivets in it! And you've wound up with a car that is missing a rivet a time or two yourselves. We all do that. But that poor fellow gets a coffee break twice a day. The rest of the time he has twenty-seven seconds to do that job and handle that machine.

He is the worker, and he hopes someday he can have a little hospital care, he can have a little pension, he can have a little social security, he can have a place to take Molly and the babies when he retires. That is his great love. His boys go to war; they fight to preserve this system. He likes his boss and he respects him. He believes in free enterprise, and he does not hate the man who makes a reasonable return.

Hartford, Connecticut
September 28, 1964

A good Congress is measured by laws that mean something to people—p-e-e-p-u-l, p-e-e-p-u-l, p-e-e-p-u-l—you know what I'm talkin' about, just plain folks.

Newark, New Jersey
October 7, 1966

But I like happy people. I like smiling faces. I like people who love their country and who believe in it, and who look forward to living in the year 2000, when the average income of a family will be $15,000 a year; when we will cross the oceans on top of the water and under the water with our cargo, when we will have a new world opening up to us in the space field.

Oh, it is such a wonderful, hopeful prospect that now I am trying to get the doctors to find out how they can control heart disease, and cancer, and stroke, and all the things that kill men early. I want to be around in the year 2000 to enjoy it, and I know I am going to enjoy it if I am here.

Butte, Montana
October 12, 1964

XVIII. LET A HUNDRED FLOWERS FLOURISH

We will have differences. . . . Even in our own country we do not see everything alike. If we did, we would all want the same wife —and that would be a problem, wouldn't it!

Washington, D.C.
February 11, 1964

We have always welcomed dissent. We have never muzzled disagreement. Pick up any afternoon paper and you will see proof of that.

Miami, Florida
February 27, 1964

I haven't come here tonight to say anything ugly about my opponent, sling any mud, do any muckraking, talk about anybody. I don't hate anyone. I try to love everybody. I "love thy neighbor as thyself," and I hope you do, too.

Pasadena, Texas
November 2, 1964

I have no doubt that freedom is going to survive and democracy is going to win. But we are not going to win by talking about each other, and using a lot of ugly names, and slinging a lot of mud, and chewing on each other. America cannot win by dividing brother against brother, sister against sister; we must have a united America—united we stand; divided we fall.

Indianapolis, Indiana
October 8, 1964

Now, sometimes they try to get me involved in personalities. But we don't need name-calling and we don't need slander and we don't need libels and we don't need labels. You really don't gain much by getting into personalities and talking about a man or his wife or his dogs on a personal basis.

Washington, D.C.
August 3, 1965

I don't believe in characterizing people with labels. I think you do a great disservice when you engage in name-calling. We want honest, forthright discussion in this country, and that will be a discussion with differences of views, and we welcome what our friends have to say, whether they agree with us or not. And I would not want to label people who agree with me or disagree with me.

News conference
Washington, D.C.
April 27, 1965

There will be some Nervous Nellies and some who will become frustrated and bothered and break ranks under the strain. And some will turn on their leaders and on their country and on our fighting men. There will be times of trial and tensions in the days ahead that will exact the best that is in all of us.

Chicago, Illinois
May 17, 1966

Now, let's look at some other education we're getting from protesting and expressing dissent in this country: During a week a short time ago our newspapers, our TV programs and our radio commentators informed us fully about the protesters and the peaceniks who invaded the Pentagon. They came there to stay. They walked over the tulips. They sat down on the steps. They slept in the halls. . . . Unfortunately a student carrying a sign, or a protester wearing a beard, or an attention seeker burning a draft card in front of a camera, can get more attention and more billing than all 10,000 of these [armed forces] volunteers.

Baltimore, Maryland
June 27, 1967

Put away all the childish divisive things, if you want the maturity and the unity that is the mortar of a nation's greatness.

I do not think that those men who are out there fighting for us tonight think we should enjoy the luxury of fighting each other back home.

Chicago, Illinois
May 17, 1966

I believe it very damaging to the American nation to have opposition for opposition's sake, and to have blind opposition. It grieves me when I see measures that are calculated to benefit all Americans opposed along party lines. . . . I try to keep as far away from partisanship and campaigning as I can.

News conference
Washington, D.C.
April 18, 1964

I almost put off my physical examination the other day because I watched these conmentators and I read these various analytical pieces by some of the ablest men in the country that I had known well for many years. I was afraid my blood pressure would be too high to have an examination at that time.

Atlantic City, New Jersey
August 28, 1964

So, if we can just restrain ourselves from eating on each other, if we can just refuse to join in tearing each other to pieces, if we can just point out the good things about our land, our country and our system, instead of indulging in cheap, mudslinging, personal politics, then America will not only be the land of the free, but it will be the land of the prosperous and the land of the brave and the land of the free.

Cleveland, Ohio
June 17, 1964

Sure we make mistakes. But point them out and we will correct them. Let's not throw the baby out, though, with the dishes.

Washington, D.C.
June 22, 1967

You would hardly expect a man who had an automobile for sale to tell you that the motor heated, that wheels had not been put on properly, that the horn wouldn't blow, that the automobile itself had a very short life, and then expect you to buy it.

But we hear other nations say so many things about our own in criticism and we say so many things ourselves that I sometimes wonder if the rest of the world hears only what's wrong with America. It's good that we have a system where we can freely talk about what's wrong because when we have the proper information we make the proper judgments.

Baltimore, Maryland
June 27, 1967

There are always critics around imploring the President to stick to the facts and not to go crystal-gazing. Some of them tell me to try to keep my feet on the ground, if not my head in the sand.

Washington, D.C.
April 17, 1964

Freedom prospers through the fair discussion of honest differences, both at home and abroad. We invite and we welcome such discussions.

But neither at home nor abroad is there any need for twisted arguments that would damage the good name of our country. The American people have little sympathy for those abroad who seek political gain from baseless denunciation of the United States, because we have helped others and because we are a leader for peace. And they will equally reject such tactics if they are employed at home.

St. Louis, Missouri
February 14, 1964

I don't resent the ugly things that have been said or the personal things, or the mud-slinging, or the name-calling, or the epithets that have been applied to me. Most people understand that when folks get desperate they are not always careful, cautious, prudent, and wise, and they do waste everybody's time by talking about these matters. But they are not going to—they may enjoy it and get their own blood pressure up and feel a peculiar sensation, but if they can just keep on talking, maybe we won't have to keep on traveling so much.

I am going to try to look at it as objectively as I can. I am going to try to really do what the Good Book advocates, "God, forgive them for they really know not what they do." I do get a little disappointed.

Cleveland, Ohio
October 8, 1964

So if you came out to meet me tonight to hear about my fears, you are going to be disappointed. If you came out to hear me speak like I had a martyr complex and nobody loves me, you are going to be disappointed, because I think that we have the greatest system of government in the world and I am proud of it. If you came out to hear me talk about all the things wrong, you are going home sad, because there are some things wrong, but the things that are right outnumber them a great deal.

Manchester, New Hampshire
September 28, 1964

All the world looks to this nation for its future, for the leadership that is required at this moment. And we cannot give that leadership and we cannot offer it if we are split up in guerrilla groups chewing on each other.

Washington, D.C.
August 10, 1964

I have never discussed with a human being something he should say or shouldn't say on Vietnam. I think debate's healthy. It's good for us, provided it's responsible.

News conference
LBJ Ranch, Texas
March 20, 1965

There is no Senator that Washington respects more, and none that the nation needs more, and none that your President values more, than Frank Church.

Boise, Idaho
October 12, 1964

Okay Frank, next time you need a dam in Idaho, ask Walter Lippmann for one.

Quoted in *Esquire*
August, 1967

Sometimes, though, we do find that our own people must endure tests and must be tried and must defend freedom, not only against enemies without, but against folks who don't understand within.

Washington, D.C.
March 1, 1965

You know, when you're milking a cow and you have all that foamy white milk in the bucket and you're just about through when all of a sudden the cow switches her tail through a pile of manure and slaps it into that foamy white milk. That's Bill Fulbright.

Quoted in *Newsweek*
September 4, 1967

Now you are stockholders in this Government, and every time you hit me—I am the only President you have got—you make me a little bit weaker to do the things that you have hired me to do. I don't expect to muffle criticism. Every one of you say we invite free speech in our country and we want free speech and we want criticism—

don't you? Every one of you do. But there is a limit to how much you want, and there is a ceiling on how much is good for you.

Washington, D.C.
April 27, 1964

So I warn you and I plead of you, if you have any suggestions or any views, or any differences, with your President—and all of you do at times, we don't see everything alike or we would all want the same wife—but communicate them to me through Uncle Sam, or Western Union, or directly, or through your friends. Don't send them through my intelligence bulletin via Peking or Hanoi or Moscow.

Washington, D.C.
May 3, 1965

And I hope if you do what you think is right, that somehow or other it is the same thing that I think is right. But if it is not, I won't question your patriotism, I won't question your Americanism, I won't question your ancestry. I may quietly in the sanctity of our bedroom whisper to Lady Bird my own personal opinion about your judgment.

New Orleans, Louisiana
October 9, 1964

Words wound. But as a veteran of twelve years in the United States Senate, I happily attest that they do not kill.

Denver, Colorado
August 26, 1966

XIX. CULTURE AND THE ARTS

Well, I am interested in the glories of art and architecture and the finer things of life and education, but I am also interested in income taxes, because that is what we use to pay for these things.

Washington, D.C.
April 13, 1965

History has shown that, if we are to achieve the Great Society for which we are all working, it is essential that the arts grow and flourish.

Washington, D.C.
August 18, 1964

No act of Congress or Executive order can call a great musician or poet into existence. But we can stand on the sidelines and cheer.

Washington, D.C.
December 2, 1964

One thing I wanted to tell you, a thing I like so much about Montana, and something that is a precious heritage to all of us, is that great artist that you had there for so many years, Charles Russell. I have one of his paintings hanging in my office, and I asked them to bring it out here because I wanted to give you just a little touch of Montana this morning.

Washington, D.C.
April 17, 1964

I spent the weekend with a delightful friend who is an artist, and I have one of his pictures in there on my wall—it is pioneers going across the country in a covered wagon. His name is Peter Hurd, and he lives in New Mexico. But that picture that is hanging in the President's office is one he painted when he was on a WPA project. And of course that project permitted him to survive. And now he is painting one of the President of the United States for pay—much more than he got on WPA.

Washington, D.C.
August 4, 1965

Mr. Peter Hurd and Mrs. Hurd are here from New Mexico spending the weekend with us. They'll be going back when they have had enough of it.

LBJ Ranch, Texas
August 1, 1965

There is, I think, a growing appreciation in America for the arts and a growing understanding and I think there is a growing demand among our people.

Washington, D.C.
August 4, 1965

That's the ugliest thing I ever saw.

To Peter Hurd about portrait
Quoted in *The New York Times*
January 6, 1967

Who the hell is Lana Turner?

Quoted in *Time*
June 22, 1953

I want to especially thank Jerry Finkelstein, Eddie Weisl, Jr., Martin Davis and his staff, Hy Brown and his staff, and Kirk Douglas and my very dear friend Gregory Peck, and Mitch Miller, Tony Bennett, Diahann Carroll, Bob Merrill, Connie Francis, Jill St. John, and all of the many others who had such a part in making this such a delightful evening. Thank you from the bottom of our hearts.

New York, New York
October 31, 1964

XX. EDUCATION AND SELF-CULTIVATION

I hope you will have it written for your children and your grandchildren to see, when they take the roster that is here today: so far as those ancient enemies are concerned—ignorance—we came, we saw, we conquered!

Washington, D.C.
March 1, 1965

My daughter Luci is very interested in science—not political science either, although she adapts herself where necessary to it. She has just been admitted to Georgetown to enter nursing school there, and she is very attracted by that possibility. When I told her this morning that I was going to meet with you today, she congratulated me.

I have forgotten just how she put it but she said something like this: "Daddy, there is just nothing more 'in' than brains."

To winners of science talent search.
Washington, D.C.
March 1, 1965

I graduated from the Johnson City High School in a class of six. For some time I had felt that my father was not really as smart as I thought he ought to be, and I thought that I could improve on a good many of my mother's approaches to life. So when I got my high school diploma I decided to follow the old philosopher Horace Greeley's advice and "Go West, young man," and seek my fortune.

With $26 in my pocket and a T-model Ford automobile, five of my schoolmates and I started out early one Saturday morning on our way to the Golden West, the great state of California. We got there in due time, minus most of my $26, and I got a very well-paying job of $90 a month running an elevator. But I found at the end of the month, after I paid for three meals and paid for my room and my laundry that I was probably better off back there eating Mama's food than I was in California.

So I went back to Texas and I got a job with the Highway Department. We didn't have to get to work until sunup, we got to quit every night at sundown. We did have to go to work on our own time. We had to be at work at sunup, and that was usually twenty or thirty miles down the road, and we had to ride home on our own time after sundown. I got the magnificent salary of a dollar a day.

After a little over a year of that, I began to think that my father's advice that I should go and take some more training and not be a school dropout—maybe he was wiser than I had thought a year before. In other words, he became a lot smarter while I was gone in California. And with the help of the good

Lord, and with a mother persistently urging me to go back to school and get some training, I hitchhiked fifty miles to get back into the classroom, where I spent four years. And I have been reasonably well employed ever since. I now have a contract that runs until January 20, 1965.

Denver, Colorado
October 12, 1964

You really should know that this Cabinet Room is called the Alumni Room of the White House, because at this table the heads of our departments and agencies gather together the roster of various alma maters that is quite imposing. We have Rhodes Scholars and numerous Phi Beta Kappas and former deans of Harvard and graduates of Yale and men from Princeton and California, and neither last nor least, Southwest Texas State Teachers College.

Washington, D.C.
March 25, 1965

I hold an honorary degree from Brown University, and I have had a very warm feeling for that institution, and particularly for President Keeney, which I formed through Senator Green, who is a member of the board of trustees there. I hope to be able to call on them. They asked me last spring to come see Senator Green and speak at the university. I agreed to it if the good Lord was willing and the creeks didn't rise.

News conference
Washington, D.C.
September 21, 1964

So I implore you to recognize before it is too late that while the Soviet Union can put up Sputnik I, and while we are debating about it, Sputnik II is saying "Beep, beep, beep," in the sky, that we are sometimes mighty slow to start, but mighty hard to stop. We don't need argumentation about the desirability of preparing our children to think and to act with judgment.

But remember, whether it is the man that picks up the telephone on the end of the "hot line" that is calling from Moscow, or whether it is the man that sits there with the responsibility of his thumb close to that button, who must act on a moment's notice, that no man's judgment on any given question is any better than the information he has on that question. And he can't get all the information he needs in this space age hunting and fishing. He can't get all that he needs on the football field or the baseball diamond. He has to get it in grade school, high school, in college, in graduate work, because Americans must never be second to anyone.

Boca Raton, Florida
October 25, 1964

I only wish that my college teacher could be here to see what is happening now. Because in my first term in college, when I made the debating team as a freshman—which was slightly unusual—when I got my grade cards my teacher gave me the lowest grade I ever received in college, and in just the course that you would expect him to give it to me in. He gave me a *D* in argumentation!

Washington, D.C.
August 3, 1965

Your state universities are playing a very critically important role in the revitalization of these states. I hope you play more. I hope that you just shovel up your knowledge to where the Governor chokes on it and where that information is available to his administrators who need your help.

To State University presidents
Washington, D.C.
August 13, 1964

And ask yourself tonight whether you want your grade-school Florida boys, and you want your high-school Florida girls, competing with the ruthless Communists who have Ph.D.'s, and expect them to out-produce them, to outthink them, and to out-lead them.

Boca Raton, Florida
October 25, 1964

And I think you can truly say in the years to come, that on this day of February—the twenty-ninth, is it? March the first? On this day, March first, Monday, is it?—on this day, March the first, I sat in the White House at 6:10, and along with my colleagues from all over the nation, I participated in the meeting and in the conference that gave America leadership in preparing the minds of her little ones.

Washington, D.C.
March 1, 1965

XXI. CONTAGIOUS OPTIMISM

This nation, this government, this administration have no foes in the capitals of the free world.

Washington, D.C.
June 9, 1965

Nowhere are views from other lands and other peoples more respected than in this White House.

Washington, D.C.
July 22, 1965

. . . There is nothing that restores a President's soul more than a warm Detroit greeting.

Detroit, Michigan
May 22, 1964

It's going to be the time, as I said, when we have a job for everyone who is willing to work, and he is going to be paid a decent wage. It's the time when every false distinction—of what your race is or your creed is or your sex or how you spell your name or where your folks came from or how you pray—it's going to be a time when none of that makes any difference.

Pittsburgh, Pennsylvania
October 27, 1964

I am happy to be here in this great city where the American Legion has its headquarters. I know what the Legion has done to maintain our vigilance in the struggle against communism.

Indianapolis, Indiana
October 8, 1964

There is not a boy in that crowd that wouldn't gallantly march down to that railroad station and put on that khaki uniform if he thought this flag was in danger tomorrow.

Columbia, South Carolina
October 26, 1964

There is less hate, there is less bigotry, there is less prejudice, there is less jealousy, there is less partisanship in your Congress among your members of the House and Senate than any time that I know of in the 35 years that I have been here.

Washington, D.C.
May 25, 1965

The dole is dead. The pork barrel is gone.

Washington, D.C.
March 9, 1965

For the first time in America's history, poverty is on the run. . . .

Washington, D.C.
April 17, 1964

The Chinese Communist nuclear detonation is a reflection of policies which do not serve the cause of peace. But there is no reason to fear that it will lead to immediate dangers of war. The nations of the free world recognize its limited significance and will persevere in their determination to preserve their independence.

Washington, D.C.
October 16, 1964

The United States and the Soviet Union still have an agenda of unresolved differences, some of them quite serious. I believe we can settle these disputes honorably and peacefully.

Quoted in *Amerika* (U.S.I.A.)
September, 1966

I told the Governor [of Alabama] that the brutality in Selma last Sunday just must not be repeated. He agreed that he abhorred brutality and regretted any instance in which any American citizen met with violence.

News conference
Washington, D.C.
March 13, 1965

There is no delegation in the United States Congress that has contributed more to the success of that Congress, that has contributed more sound, constructive leadership to the entire Nation, than the great State of Arkansas.

Texarkana, Texas-Arkansas
September 25, 1964

I have just talked to Mr. J. Edgar Hoover, head of the Federal Bureau of Investigation. He assures me that the investigation in Mississippi is going exceedingly well; that substantive results can be expected in a very short period of time.

News conference
LBJ Ranch, Texas
August 8, 1964

I believe Georgia will join with the entire nation to insure that every man enjoys all the rights secured him by the American Constitution.

Atlanta, Georgia
May 8, 1964

The whole nation can take heart from the fact that there are those in the South who believe in justice in racial matters and who are determined not to stand for acts of violence and terror.

Austin, Texas
December 3, 1965

Americans have no patience with mixing politics and medicine and there is going to be none of that.

Our American medical profession is the best that the world has ever known. Our only purpose is to help that profession, never to harass it.

Washington, D.C.
August 18, 1964

The speed and effectiveness with which our Nation's defense industry has responded to this challenge is not surprising, but it is gratifying. The contractors engaged in this important effort have pledged a dollar's value for every dollar spent, and this value is being reflected in lower costs to the American people for their national defense.

Washington, D.C.
April 28, 1965

I don't think anyone seriously believes that we have destroyed the will to work or the will to produce.

Oklahoma City, Oklahoma
September 25, 1964

I expect the leaders of the labor workers' movement in this country to come up, punch that timeclock, stay on that shift until we preserve democracy for ourselves and for free people all around the globe.

Washington, D.C.
May 3, 1965

So I say to you young business leaders of America, there never has been a time when the business groups of this country, the young leaders of this country, the employees and the labor leaders of this country have cooperated with their Government more than now. And your President's grateful for it.

Baltimore, Maryland
June 27, 1967

. . . I am confident that the "See the United States" program will be successful and I urge both American citizens and citizens of other countries to travel whenever they can throughout our beautiful country.

News conference
Washington, D.C.
August 15, 1964

I have every reason to believe that we'll be successful [in Vietnam], that a stable democratic society will be built.

News conference
Washington, D.C.
April 22, 1966

No, I don't think that the teach-ins and the differences of opinion have increased the strength of the North Vietnamese or the aggression that's taking place.

News conference
Washington, D.C.
July 13, 1965

Somehow or other, optimist that I am, I just believe that peace is coming nearer.

Seattle, Washington
September 16, 1964

Tomorrow will be drastically different from today.

Washington, D.C.
April 17, 1964

XXII. GRATITUDE

Since World War II we have spent a hundred billion dollars trying to help other people. When I drove down the streets of Rome, people ran out and stopped my car and said, "Look at that skyline, that industrial activity back there. Except for the help of Americans, we would have never made it. Never before in the history of civilization had the victors treated the vanquished as you have treated us, and we want you to go back and thank Americans."

So, regardless of what you hear and regardless of what some of the bellyachers say, we are a much beloved people throughout the world. We are respected and we appreciate it.

Washington, D.C.
February 11, 1964

One of the most stimulating and inspiring experiences of my entire public life occurred to me on the streets of Rome just a few months ago when I was Vice President and I was driving down the streets of that beautiful city.

A priest came running from his schoolroom, followed by other teachers, and three or four hundred little boys. He had seen the American flag flying on the Vice President's car.

He threw himself in front of this car and the brakes had to take a screeching halt, and we came to a stop. He dashed up to the door and he said, "I just could not let the American flag go by, because never in the history of all mankind have any people demonstrated so much compassion and so much humaneness. Never have the victors treated the vanquished as the United States has treated us."

And then he turned and looked at the Rome skyline that had been rebuilt since World War II, and he pointed to the magnificent buildings that towered that skyline, and to the smokestacks where industry was thriving, and he said, "There, together we rebuilt this land. I want you to go back and on behalf of the four hundred little children in my school, say thank you to all the people of the United States for the sacrifices they made in order that we could build again."

El Paso, Texas
September 25, 1964

When I drove down the streets of Rome just a few months ago, a priest ran out and threw himself in front of my car. And he had four hundred little boys following him. He said, "We want you to thank America—

America. It is the only land in the world where the victors would treat the vanquished as you have treated us. You defeated us in war and then you came to help us rebuild. Look at that skyline and look at those people working, and look at the happiness on these children's faces. That must make you feel mighty good, that you have that much Christianity in your country."

Manchester, New Hampshire
September 28, 1964

Not long ago I was driving down the streets of Naples, and a young priest dashed and threw himself in front of my car. He had four hundred boys in his school. He said: "Please, Mr. Vice President, can I give you a message for America? Please tell the American people that never in all the history of the world has the victor treated the vanquished as America treated Italy. You extended the hand of friendship and helped to rebuild our cities. You look at that beautiful skyline of buildings," and he pointed to buildings like these. "You helped rebuild those buildings. Today our people are a prosperous people, and we honor and we revere and we love America."

San Francisco, California
October 11, 1964

I have had many memorable visits in Italy.

Washington, D.C.
February 26, 1965

XXIII. WHITE MAN'S BURDEN

On every continent and in every land to which Mrs. Johnson and I traveled, we found faith and hope and love toward this land of America and toward our people.

Washington, D.C.
January 8, 1964

Let's just see if we can't find something good about America, and let's see if we can't take a little pride in that flag, and let's see if we can't have a little feeling well up in us and see if we can't get down on our knees sometime during the night and thank God that I am an American.

I have traveled around the world and I have been in many countries, and I have seen the glories of art and architecture. I have seen the sun rise on Mont Blanc. But the most beautiful vision that these eyes ever beheld was that American flag in a foreign land.

San Diego, California
October 28, 1964

. . . Oh, you just don't know until you talk to the leaders of 114 other nations how much you have got to be grateful for; how much you have got to be proud of!

Washington, D.C.
May 3, 1965

We are going to make life better and more enjoyable and more significant for all the 3 billion people of the world. We've got a moral duty, a Christian duty, to help our neighbors.

Washington, D.C.
July 14, 1965

And as I told you in our last meeting, I plead with my Cabinet—every time I see 'em, I say to Secretary McNamara, "You be sure that our men have the morale and have the equipment and have the necessary means of seeing that we keep our commitments in Vietnam. And we have the strength to do it. And Mr. Rusk, while he's working with his right hand on strength and stability there and doing the job we're committed to do, you and Mr. Goldberg and the rest of you use that left hand and be sure that you do everything to get us away from the battlefield and back at the conference table, if that's possible." So we're like a man in the ring—we're using our right and our left constantly.

News conference
Washington, D.C.
August 25, 1965

. . . And the one thing that sustains me most is to see what we are doing for the lame and the palsied, what we are doing in adding knowledge in the field of education, what we are doing in conservation and beautification to make this a more beautiful land, and to make this not just "America the Beautiful," but the "World the Beautiful."

Bethesda, Maryland
August 9, 1965

The people of the world, I think, prefer reasoned agreement to ready attack. That is why we must follow the Prophet Isaiah many, many times before we send the Marines, and say, "Come now, let us reason together."

Washington, D.C.
March 24, 1964

The American people hadn't elected their President to dodge and duck and refuse to face up to the unpleasant.

Since that time we have evacuated 2,500 Americans. The Michigan State University jazz band was down there [in the Dominican Republic]. We got them home. The brewers—the brewery people—I guess they didn't know you all were meeting here in Washington, they were having their convention down there, and we got them home. . . . We have 5,000 nationals from thirty other countries and Americans yet to be evacuated from Santo Domingo and all of the countryside. We will by tonight have 14,000 Americans there to get that job done.

Washington, D.C.
May 3, 1965

Since that time we have evacuated approximately 3,000 persons. It has been necessary for a few Marines to go out and take an old lady and her little belongings and with a crippled hip, carry her down through the streets where the firing is taking place and finally get her to a boat. But we have carried 3,000 that way without the loss of a single civilian up to now.

Washington, D.C.
May 4, 1965

So let's go home tonight and let's don't weep on our pillow. Let's say our prayers and thank our good Lord Almighty that we are as lucky as we are, and that we enjoy the blessings that are ours.

Oklahoma City, Oklahoma
September 25, 1964

Of course we act out of enlightened self-interest. We are a nation responsible to our people. But the pages of history can be searched in vain for another power whose pursuit of that self-interest was so infused with grandeur of spirit and morality of purpose.

New York, New York
October 14, 1964

Luci told me, "There is no use of your going out there, I have already been to Dayton." But I said, "Wouldn't it really be better for us, wouldn't it be better for the Soviet Union, wouldn't it be better for Great

Britain, wouldn't it be better for Germany, wouldn't it be better for all the people of the world who are looking to us for leadership if we carried Ohio by 400,000 instead of 300,000?"

Dayton, Ohio
October 16, 1964

XXIV. MARTYRDOM AND SACRIFICE

Now I am the most denounced man in the world. All the Communist nations have a regular program on me that runs twenty-four hours a day. Some of the non-Communist nations just kind of practice on me. And occasionally I get touched up here at home in the Senate and the House of Representatives. But that is not important. . . .

Washington, D.C.
May 3, 1965

. . . Nothing really seems to go right from early in the morning till late at night. . . . Sometimes late at night when I am tired and I read what someone has said about me during the day, I am inclined to respond.

Washington, D.C.
March 1, 1965

And one of the greatest satisfactions that come to me in my hours of sunshine and sorrow, and my nights of trouble, is the knowledge that my daughter [Luci] who is a part of you, has decided to spend her life healing the sick and ministering to the needs of the needy.

Commencement exercises
National Cathedral School
Washington, D.C.
June 1, 1965

I especially appreciate your coming here because I feel that I have a rapport with you and they won't let me get out of the gate so I am glad they let you in.

To White House visitors
Washington, D.C.
May 14, 1965

Sometimes in the late of night, when all the Capital City has gone to sleep, I sit by myself behind that big black fence and I read and I think. And oftentimes it is so quiet in the White House that I can almost hear the footsteps of the men who have lived in that house, and the men who have walked its halls and have slept in its rooms, and have stayed awake waiting for the sun to come up—Jefferson, Madison, Jackson, Abraham Lincoln, Theodore Roosevelt, Woodrow Wilson, Franklin D. Roosevelt, Harry Truman, Dwight Eisenhower, and John Fitzgerald Kennedy.

Texarkana, Texas-Arkansas
September 25, 1964

I must say, a time or two when I have turned on a television spot or have turned on my car radio, I have heard some rather uncomplimentary comments about the President, and for a moment it distressed me some. But when I got back home and I looked back over what they had said about Washington, Jefferson, Jackson, Abraham Lincoln—Abraham Lincoln said he went back to his hometown and no one there spoke to him except one woman and she seemed to wish she could have avoided it. I remember what they said about Wilson, Roosevelt, Eisenhower and Kennedy.

Akron, Ohio
October 21, 1964

You are here in the White House Rose Garden. We have beautiful roses on all sides of you here. The thorns are all in the next office, to the right.

Washington, D.C.
April 21, 1964

XXV. HUMBLE ORIGINS OF THE PEOPLE'S SERVANT

Yes, Government is the son of a tenant farmer from Texas who is speaking to you tonight.

Boy Scout Jamboree
Valley Forge, Pennsylvania
July 23, 1964

I have a little house where I was born, the son of a tenant farmer, a picture of which is hanging up in my bedroom, because every night when I go to bed and every morning when I wake up, I call it the "opportunity house."

Washington, D.C.
April 27, 1964

What other system would permit the son of a tenant farmer who was born in a three-room house fifty-six years ago to become President of the land?

Washington, D.C.
February 5, 1965

I have taken a long journey from a tenant farm in West Texas to this platform in Madison Square Garden.

New York, New York
October 31, 1964

My roots are deeper in the soil than most Presidents' have been. I am proud to be the son of a tenant farmer; I am proud of land of my own. I love that land. I think I know what farmers want and what they need.

Des Moines, Iowa
October 7, 1964

It was here, as a barefoot boy around my daddy's desk in that great hall of the House of Representatives where he served for six terms and where my grandfather served ahead of him, that I first learned that Government is not an enemy of the people.

Austin, Texas
November 2, 1964

My earliest memories of my father go back practically to my infancy. But the one I remember best was the way he used to hustle me out of a warm bed into a cold morning. "Get up, Lyndon, get up!" he would shout. "Every boy in town has an hour's head start on you already."

Quoted in *Parade*
January 5, 1964

Oh, what a wonderful morning! My, what a wonderful day!

Back in my boyhood, we had breakfast at home on Sunday morning, then we went down the road to church, then we had dinner-on-the-ground in front of the Pedernales River.

This morning we had breakfast at home in Texas, we flew out by jet and went to church in Arizona, and now we have come all the way out to the shores of the Pacific to have dinner-on-the-ground.

South Gate, California
October 11, 1964

I had my teacher Sunday who taught me when I was four years old. She is now in her seventies and she is still young and pretty as a daisy. . . . But when I was four years old—they wouldn't let us enter until six, but she broke the rule and held me on one knee and held another little friend of mine named Hugo Kline on the other knee. We located Hugo the other day—he is a barber up in Fredericksburg. . . .

Washington, D.C.
April 13, 1965

I grew up on land like this back in Texas. I am going back to it when I finish here this evening. That land is thin soil and scrub oak and blackjack trees. The Pedernales River that runs in front of my little farmhouse was just a trickle in the dry season, but when the rains came down from the hills the Pedernales always drowned all of us.

Eufaula, Oklahoma
September 25, 1964

When I was young, I often walked out after supper and looked up at the scattered Texas sky. As a boy, on those still nights, I wondered what those heavens had seen, what they would see, and what they might bring to me.

The world has turned many times since then, but still in the evening I sometimes walk out and look across the great Capital City where I live, and I dream the same dreams, and I ask the same questions.

Detroit, Michigan
September 7, 1964

Forty years ago, almost to this very night, I left my high-school diploma at home and I headed West to seek the fame and fortune that I knew America offered. About 20 months later, I came back, back to Johnson City, with empty hands and empty pockets. I came back because I realized that the place to really begin was the place that I had been all the time.

Commencement address
Johnson City, Texas, High School
May 29, 1964

All my life I have drawn sustenance from the rivers and from the hills of my native state. I do not see them so often any more these days, and I am lonesome for them almost constantly. But their message of love and challenge is written in my spirit. I want no less for all the children of America than what I was privileged to have as a boy.

Portland, Oregon
September 17, 1964

All my life, I have drawn sustenance from the rivers and hills of my native state. I do not see them so often any more. I am lonesome for them almost constantly. But their message of love and challenge is written in my spirit. I want no less for all the children of America.

Sacramento, California
September 17, 1964

. . . All my life I have drawn strength, and something more, from those Texas hills. Sometimes, in the highest councils of the Nation, in this house, I sit back and I can almost feel that rough, unyielding, sticky clay soil between my toes, and it stirs memories that often give me comfort and sometimes give me a pretty firm purpose.

Washington, D.C.
May 25, 1965

Because I'm from below the Mason-Dixon line . . . you think we all have tobacco juice on our shirts.

To reporters during campaign, 1960

XXVI. COSMOPOLITANISM

I feel so good this morning and you have a lot to do with it. This little state of Delaware all through the years has had a very special spot in my heart, because the people that I have known that have lived here are very much like my people.

Dover, Delaware
October 31, 1964

When I come to Georgia, it is like coming home. My roots are deep in Georgia. Georgia has given me much to be proud of. Georgia has given much to this nation's progress, and there is a great deal more yet to be done.

Augusta, Georgia
October 26, 1964

There is something about this Florida air, clean and alive, that reminds me of Texas. There is much similarity between Texas and Florida that has nothing to do with oranges and grapefruit, but it has to do with people and climate. The sun is warm, the people are friendly, and the tomorrows are always bright with hope.

Boca Raton, Florida
October 25, 1964

Idaho's potatoes are wonderful, but Idaho can produce greater treasures for America in the lives and in the minds of Idaho's sons and daughters.

Boise, Idaho
October 12, 1964

California sets a fine example for the nation, because here Americans and Texans live together side by side in relative harmony.

Your state was almost my home state, too.

When I was a teenager, I heard that California wanted men to match her mountains, so I came out here to apply. But I got a job in the fruit orchards instead and I went back home to the Texas hills.

Sacramento, California
September 17, 1964

But I do want you to know since I was a little boy that went to the post office in the general store, the first time, and put on my first pair of Buster Brown shoes that were made here in St. Louis, I have always had great faith in the people of Missouri.

St. Louis, Missouri
October 21, 1964

So many of my ancestors come from Kentucky that I can sing "My Old Kentucky Home" with almost as much feeling as you.

Louisville, Kentucky
October 9, 1964

I have been to Wyoming a number of times. I like your white-faced Herefords. I like your cowmen. I know your oilmen.

Casper, Wyoming
October 12, 1964

As I will return tonight to my large room and my lonely desk in the White House, to cope with the decisions that have come to that desk through the day from all countries of the world, and when I review the problems of our men in uniform and those on strike, when I see the farmer and the laborer seeking justice and believing that his Government will do what is right, my mind will wander back here to the little state of Rhode Island, far away from what was once the largest state in the Nation where I was born.

Providence, Rhode Island
September 28, 1964

I can tell you this, and it is no secret, and it is not off the record: The West is on the move. The West is the "Go-go" section of America.

Las Vegas, Nevada
October 11, 1964

XXVII. PIETY AND CORRECT EXAMPLE

Well, I am against sin, and I am against lawlessness, and I am very much opposed to violence. I think we have to put a stop to it.

News conference
Washington, D.C.
July 24, 1964

I am not a theologian. I am not a philosopher. I am just a public servant that is doing the very best I know how. But in more than three decades of public life, I have seen firsthand how basic spiritual beliefs and deeds can shatter barriers of politics and bigotry. I have seen those barriers crumble in the presence of faith and hope, and from this experience I have drawn new hope that the seemingly insurmountable moral issues that we face at home and abroad today can be resolved by men of strong faith and men of brave deeds.

Washington, D.C.
March 25, 1964

Let us ask ourselves if our every act, our every public declaration and exhibition is being guided by the Golden Rule, "Do unto others as you would have them do unto you."

Washington, D.C.
August 18, 1964

These folks who think you can have government by ultimatum are wrong. You better get a little closer to Prophet Isaiah and the Good Book and "Come now, let us reason together," because there is not an ultimatum that any President can issue that could have produced one of these former governors on this platform, not a single ultimatum. You could take all the tanks in our combat divisions and all the planes in the sky, and all the Polaris missiles, and you couldn't have made a one of them come up here. But you can reason with them.

Louisville, Kentucky
October 9, 1964

This administration is going to be a compassionate administration. We believe in the Golden Rule of doing unto others as you would have them do unto you.

Washington, D.C.
January 28, 1964

Embrace those who tell you to follow the Golden Rule, do unto others as you would have them do unto you, and to love thy neighbor as thyself.

To the United Steelworkers of America
Atlantic City, New Jersey
September 22, 1964

And if I am your President I am not only going to preach the Golden Rule throughout the world and throughout this land, of do unto others as you would have them do unto you, but I am going to practice it.

Denver, Colorado
October 12, 1964

. . . The true image of Washington is not that of power or pomp or plenty. It is, rather, that of a prayerful capital of good and God-fearing people.

Washington, D.C.
February 5, 1964

I think I would have made my parents happier if at 16 or 18, or even 20, I had conducted myself to the same high standards of morals as my daughters apply to themselves now.

News conference
Washington, D.C.
April 4, 1964

Those of you who were thoughtful enough to bring me a turkey to be thankful for, I will tell you I will use that turkey in my Thanksgiving Day participation. All of you good folks—even some of you columnists that get things mixed up sometimes—I am going to use in my prayers.

Washington, D.C.
November 17, 1964

Now let's go home and have a good night's sleep and pray for each other and get up and go vote early in the morning the Democratic ticket from the courthouse to the White House.

Austin, Texas
November 2, 1964

I might even go hunting. I haven't had a chance to do that this year, and I would like to go and spend a day out in the hills, communing with myself.

News conference
Washington, D.C.
December 18, 1963

I am usually a dollar short and an hour late. But my intentions are good.

Rocky Mount, North Carolina
May 7, 1964

Dr. Billy Graham comes here frequently and gives me strength and comfort and prays over me, and nobody needs a prayer more than I do.

Washington, D.C.
April 2, 1965

I wish you could have seen Billy Graham and Bill Moyers in that pool together the other day. Everyone else was already a Christian, so they just took turns baptizing each other.

Washington, D.C.
March 25, 1964

XXVIII. DOMESTIC TRANQUILITY

I lived with two teenagers for years. . . . I kept my cool. I haven't bugged out. I'm still in Fat City.

Washington, D.C.
June 13, 1967

Someone asked me the other day about how I liked to live in the White House and they told me it was off the record. And I said, "Well, we do have our problems. We wake up early in the morning when the planes are coming back from the raids. We go to work and we come to a late lunch and, if we are lucky, we get a little nap after a bowl of soup, and get refreshed for the next part of that day from four until twelve. But sometimes I am interrupted in the nap by Lady Bird and Laurence Rockefeller, and about eighty others in the next room, talking about flowers, roadsides and so forth."

Washington, D.C.
May 25, 1965

I'm treated better than most people who work in this country. I get up early and I work till three or four o'clock in the afternoon and then I take two hours off and have a wonderful shower and shave and go to bed and sleep two hours while the rest of you people are trying to fight the traffic to get home. Then I go back at five o'clock refreshed and work until the evening. And these experiences are exciting and stimulating. I'm going to be in the house with my friends and I do always relax a little better when I'm in friendly company.

News conference
Washington, D.C.
October 13, 1966

First of all I want to thank you very much for your thoughtfulness in coming here to the White House today and bringing me a turkey to eat on Thanksgiving. I hadn't been quite sure what I was going to eat Thanksgiving, but I am glad I can eat turkey instead of crow.

Washington, D.C.
November 17, 1964

I just wish that we had as good a chance for rain down home as you have here. We have been caking our old cows all summer, and we are out of pears down there.

Oklahoma City, Oklahoma
September 25, 1964

You know, in Texas, when we go to buy a farm, we don't put too much importance on the manmade disappointments—like a rundown barn or a badly fenced pasture. A good farmer goes out to the fields and sees what's growing. He stoops down and tastes a little bit of the soil. He looks at the stock and the streams and the spring. If these are ample or can be made so by the sweat of his brow, the farmer knows the place holds a future. I grew up on that land. Some of it was mighty poor and rocky—but some of it was good. I learned not to be afraid of disappointments—of the weeds and rocks—but to value the good soil and the hard, constructive work.

Quoted in *Amerika* (U.S.I.A.)
September, 1966

Bird's an East Texan. All she likes is pork chops and candied yams.

The *Baltimore Sun*
January 6, 1964

"Greetings from the Deer Country of Texas"

We hope your holiday season will be more delectable because of our hunting season. In Texas, from November 15 on, the hills are alive with the sound of hunters. Here is the result, killed this year by our trusty rifles, on the LBJ ranch.

Should you happen to have our ingredients on hand, try our favorite recipe for—DEER MEAT SAUSAGE.

One-half deer
One-half hog
25 ounces of salt
20 ounces of black pepper
8 ounces of red pepper
2 ounces of sage

Mix together for 200 pounds of sausage.

Christmas note to friends
1963

XXIX. HEROIC EXHORTATIONS

I will tell you a little story about a boy I asked one time to come stay all night with me. His mother said no, he couldn't go. He had a little brother about twelve years old that was overweight, and we nicknamed him "Bones." Cecil was the one I wanted to stay the weekend with me, and his mother said, "No, Cecil, you can't go." Cecil kind of winked a little bit and said, "Mama, I don't think that is fair. Bones done been two wheres and I ain't been no wheres."

News conference
Washington, D.C.
March 12, 1966

I have seen on the faces of the people of this country a happiness, and a pleasure, and a satisfaction that is not always reflected in what I read.

I might be like Uncle Ezra. You know the doctor told him he had to quit drinking if he'd improve his hearing. But when he went back, the doctor said, "Well, are you still drinking?" And he said, "Yes." The doctor said, "I told you you'd have to quit it to improve your hearing." And he said, "Well, doctor," he said, "I like what I drink so much better than what I hear that I just didn't take your prescription."

News conference
Washington, D.C.
October 13, 1966

My mother used to say, "Who eats the most cornbread gets the most cake." I assume that was because we had more cornbread than cake.

News conference
Washington, D.C.
March 31, 1966

Well, I will tell you a little story before I go home. This happened down in my country. We lived out on a cotton farm when I was a boy, and we had a little boy there that left a little after lunch one day and went over to the Old Settlers' Reunion, the Old Confederate Reunion, and he didn't come back until dark that night—just about weighing-in time—just about the time we were unloading our sacks and weighing in.

And the boss said, "Where in the world have you been all afternoon?"

He said, "I have been over to the Old Confederate Reunion."

The boss said, "What did you do all afternoon at the Confederate Reunion?"

The boy said, "Well, I listened to a United States Senator make a speech."

The boss said, "Well, the Senator didn't speak all evening, did he?"

The boy said, "Mighty near, mighty near."

The boss said, "Who was the Senator and what did he speak about?"

"Well," the boy said, "Boss, his name was Senator Joseph Weldon Bailey, from Texas, and I don't recall precisely all the Senator talked about, but the general impression I got all afternoon was that he was recommending himself most highly."

Columbia, South Carolina
October 26, 1964

In my country we are very proud of what we call the Texas Rangers. Sometimes when we have a little row or misunderstanding in our country, they call out a Ranger. One of our old cowpuncher friends took some cattle up to Kansas City to sell, and one of the fellows out in the stockyards said to him, while they were waiting for the bidders to come in, "Please tell me what is really the difference between a sheriff and a Texas Ranger."

The old man, a Ranger for many years, ran his hand through his hair and deliberated, and he said, "Well, a Ranger is one that when you plug him when you hit him, he just keeps coming." And we must let the rest of the world know that we speak softly, we carry a big stick, but we have the will and the determination, and if they ever hit us it is not going to stop us—we are just going to keep coming.

Manchester, New Hampshire
September 28, 1964

XXX. ULTIMATE REFLECTION

I'm the only President you've got.

Washington, D.C.
April 27, 1964